T0049198

Voice Therapy for Children

An Instructional Manual

Voice Therapy for Children

An Instructional Manual

Estella P. M. Ma

This publication has been generously supported by Sik Sik Yuen Education Services Fund.

Hong Kong University Press
The University of Hong Kong
Pok Fu Lam Road
Hong Kong
https://hkupress.hku.hk

© 2023 Hong Kong University Press

ISBN 978-988-8754-21-2 (*Paperback*)

All rights reserved. No portion of this publication may be reproduced or transmitted in any form or by any means, electronic or mechanical, including photocopying, recording, or any information storage or retrieval system, without prior permission in writing from the publisher.

British Library Cataloguing-in-Publication Data
A catalogue record for this book is available from the British Library.

10 9 8 7 6 5 4 3 2 1

Printed and bound by Sunshine (Caimei) Printing Co., Ltd. in Hong Kong, China

To my parents and my family for encouraging
and supporting me in pursuing my academic dream,
and to my teacher and mentor,
Professor Edwin Yiu, who introduced me to the science
and art of voice research

Contents

List of Handouts

List of Diagrams

Preface

Voice disorders are common among children. A high prevalence of voice disorders has been reported in the child population, the rates ranging from at least 6% to 30.3% depending on the diagnostic methods and criteria. Behavioral (non-surgical) voice therapy is the first-line management approach for voice problems in children. Nevertheless, how well speech pathologists are prepared for managing pediatric voice caseloads has been a concern. A local survey conducted by the Hong Kong University Voice Research Laboratory with 56 practicing school-based speech pathologists in Hong Kong found that only a few (less than 10%) respondents felt very confident or totally confident in managing pediatric voice problems. The vast majority of respondents (90.6%) were less than moderately confident in managing pediatric voice caseloads (Ma, Chow, & Lam, 2022). We have regularly received requests from clinicians who seek clinical resources on pediatric voice disorders that are relevant to the Hong Kong context.

The motivation for this instructional manual arose from the recognized fact that there are very few textbooks and clinical sourcebooks on pediatric voice. The majority of textbooks provide a general description of the therapeutic technique and the underlying physiologic principles and rationale. However, practical issues and clinical tips are not usually highlighted; for example, *how to keep children engaged in the voice therapy, how to facilitate young children perform and learn the voicing technique, how to select age-appropriate practice stimuli and games*, and *how to facilitate children proceed through the hierarchy of vocal exercises*. In many instances, speech pathology students can only gain these skills and knowledge through direct contact with patients or indirectly through observing the demonstrations by their clinical educators. An instructional manual that addresses these issues is much needed for speech pathology students to learn the "how" in conducting voice therapy with children.

The Voice Research Laboratory has published the *Voice Therapy Instructional Manual* (Yiu & Ma, 2001). Although the manual provides readers with step-by-step instructions in carrying out voice therapy, it was originally developed for adult voice patients. Managing pediatric patients is very different from managing adult patients, due to different motivation, cognitive levels, and language abilities between the two populations. For example, the use of games, pictures, and analogies are needed to help children learn abstract voice concepts. Clinicians' instructions and presentations of practice stimuli are also different. The present manual, *Voice Therapy for Children: An Instructional*

Manual, aims to address the existing gap by maximizing speech pathology students' and clinicians' competence, knowledge, and effectiveness in managing pediatric voice caseloads. It is my hope that this manual will become a necessary and invaluable sourcebook for students and clinicians who seek resources to provide treatment to Cantonese-speaking children with voice disorders.

Estella P. M. Ma
February 2023

Acknowledgments

Funding for the development and evaluation of the voice therapy program described in this manual was provided by the Research Grants Council General Research Fund of the University Grants Committee (Project Grant Number: HKU 17634416). The illustrations and picture stimuli used in this manual were prepared with partial support from the HKU Faculty of Education Research Fund.

My sincere appreciation is extended to:

- Yann Lam and Grace Pang for their initial contribution to the development and validation of the voice therapy program.
- Anney Fung, Heather Lo, Billy Wong, and Sunny Wong for creating the vivid illustrations and picture stimuli.
- Sunny Wong for writing the theme song "Star of Healthy Voice" for the earlier version of the program.
- Darryl Chan, Natalie Lau, Julianne Lee, Heather Lo, and Kinny Yeung for their careful reading and excellent suggestions on early drafts of the manual.
- All children and parents who participated in the validation study of the program.

The publication of this manual would not have been possible without the generous funding support from Sik Sik Yuen Foundation. The unconditional support of Mr. Stephen Ma Chak-wa, MH CStJ (Chairman of the Sik Sik Yuen Board of Directors) and his board members for the development and advancement of voice therapy service for children in Hong Kong is gratefully acknowledged.

About the Author

Estella P. M. Ma, PhD, is an associate professor of the Faculty of Education and director of the Voice Research Laboratory at the University of Hong Kong. Her research centers on voice science and disorders, with special foci on pediatric voice, motor learning, and instrumental voice assessments. The majority of her research takes a functional perspective and is framed by the health classification scheme of the World Health Organization's International Classification of Functioning, Disability and Health (ICF). She is the co-editor of *Handbook of Voice Assessments* (2011) with Edwin M.-L. Yiu, PhD. She has served as associate editor of *Folia Phoniatrica et Logopaedica*, associate editor of *Logopedics Phoniatrics Vocology*, and an editorial board member of the *Journal of Speech, Language, and Hearing Research*. She was the vice-chair and deputy chair of the International Association of Communication Sciences and Disorders (IALP) Voice Committee from 2015 to 2021, and is currently a consultant to the committee. She is also a member of the Voice Foundation Scientific Advisory Board.

Introductory Remarks

What Is the Purpose of This Manual?

The aim of this instructional manual is to serve as a practical companion for student clinicians and entry-level speech pathologists in conducting voice therapy with children. It provides clinicians with practical verbal instructions, content, and materials for the implementation of therapy sessions with children who have voice disorders.

What Is This Manual About?

This instructional manual was originally developed as the voice therapy protocol for a research project funded by Research Grants Council General Research Fund, which aimed at evaluating voice treatment efficiency in school-age children with vocal nodules. The details of the instructions are set out to ensure a standardized protocol for minimizing variability across clinicians:

- Content: Vocal hygiene education and resonant voice therapy (also known as humming).
- Arrangement of sessions: The protocol is presented as six weekly sessions of 45 minutes each.
- Setting: The protocol is designed as group therapy with two to three children in each group. Parents/caretakers are encouraged to attend.
- Use of language: The instructions and tasks described in this manual are most relevant for school-age children.
- Type of vocal pathologies: Benign vocal fold lesions associated with phonotrauma.

What Are the Features of This Manual?

This manual has a number of unique features:

1. The manual contains detailed, step-by-step instructions for each voice therapy session. Clinicians can directly follow the detailed instructions and can immediately implement treatment with patients.
2. Practical tips and strategies for troubleshooting are highlighted at different stages of the therapy.

3. Ready-to-use clinical materials include picture cards for eliciting stimulus (essential when working with young children) and reproducible handouts for clinical use. The picture cards are accompanied with QR codes for downloading and for therapy session preparation.
4. The program described in the manual is evidence-based. This instructional manual was developed from a project funded by the Hong Kong Research Grants Council awarded to the author. The project evaluated the effectiveness of vocal hygiene education with resonant voice training for children with vocal nodules. Our results show that the program is effective in improving voice quality and quality of life in children with voice problems. More details are available in Ma, Cheung, Siu, and Lo (2021) and from the author upon request.

How to Use This Manual Most Efficiently? What Do I Need to Prepare before Using This Manual?

This manual is not intended to be an academic textbook on pediatric voice. It does not provide information on the theory and physiological underpinning of voice exercises. In order to use the manual efficiently, clinicians should have a good knowledge about laryngeal development and biomechanics in children. A good understanding of the language and cognitive level of the age group that you will be working with can also lead to success in conducting voice therapy with children. Readers can refer to Section Three of this manual for suggested references for extended reading.

Finally, clinician should exercise flexibility when implementing the voice therapy protocol. For example, clinicians can adjust the number of sessions and duration of each session according to individual cases and the corresponding clinical settings. When administering the protocol with children of other age groups, modifications may be necessary in order to match the reading level and cognitive processing level of the child. For example, the choice of games and tasks should be age appropriate. Use of technology (e.g., computer software, applications) in voice therapy can be motivating for young children. Clinicians should exercise their clinical knowledge and make adjustments accordingly.

Instructional Manual

Introduction and Vocal Hygiene

Objectives

Students will

1. demonstrate understanding of laryngeal anatomy and phonatory physiology,

2. demonstrate understanding of laryngeal pathologies associated with phonotrauma,

3. differentiate and rate good versus poor voice qualities, and

4. identify healthy and unhealthy vocal habits.

Materials

- Worksheets: Handout 1. Quiz on vocal hygiene knowledge
  Handout 2. "Star of Healthy Voice" song
  Handout 3. My healthy voice use agreement
  Handout 4. Home practice: Session 1
  Handout 5. "Star of Healthy Voice" reward chart
  Diagram 1. Laryngeal anatomy and phonatory physiology
  Diagram 2. Unhealthy vocal folds
  Diagram 3. Voice rating scale
  Diagram 4. Vocal hygiene

- Other: Folder for student to carry handouts
  Larynx model
  Ruler
  Stamp
  Device to display video and audio files
  Healthy and dysphonic voice samples
  "Star of Healthy Voice" puppet show (accessed by scanning the QR code)

Puppet Show

Session Outline

Introduction and rapport building (5 min)

"Welcome to the voice program. This program consists of 6 sessions. We'll learn how the voice is produced. We'll also learn how to achieve healthy and effective voice production."

Start the session by welcoming the students and building rapport with them. Invite the students to share how they feel about their voice and what they wish to achieve from this program. Create a positive and collaborative atmosphere to promote therapy success.

"Before we start, could each of you share with us 'How would you describe your voice?', 'How do you feel about your voice?', 'Does your voice affect your communication with your family and friends?' and 'What do you want to learn from this program?'" (The clinician can pay attention to students' voice qualities when they speak.)

Voice production mechanism and common voice problems (15 min)

"First, let's talk about how the voice is produced. The vocal folds are responsible for making sounds. Does anyone know where the vocal folds are?"

Help the students to realize the location of the vocal folds by placing the palm over the thyroid notch (that is, the Adam's apple) and say /a/ for a few seconds. Ask them to feel the vibration during phonation.

引言（5分鐘）

「歡迎參加聲線治療課程。此課程一共有六堂。我們會學習聲線是如何發出的，亦會一起練習正確而有效的用聲方法。」

「課程開始之前，我想邀請每一位學員講出你叫甚麼名字，然後跟大家分享：你會怎樣形容你的聲線？你希望從這個課程中得著甚麼？」（言語治療師可從中留意學生的聲線質素和發聲方法）

發聲原理及常見聲線問題（15分鐘）

「今日我們會探討聲線是如何發出的。聲線主要是靠聲帶振動而發出。你們知道聲帶在哪裡嗎？」

Diagram 1.
Laryngeal anatomy and phonatory physiology

圖1.
發聲原理

"There's a pair of vocal folds sitting in the larynx. Imagine peeling off the skin around your neck. You'll see the larynx. (Show students the larynx model.) Here are the vocal folds. (Point out where the vocal folds are.) They're controlled by nerves and muscles within and around the larynx. The vocal folds work in pairs to produce the voice."

「我們的喉嚨裡有一對好朋友：聲帶。幻想把頸部周圍的皮剝掉，你們會看見自己的喉嚨，像這個模型一樣。(給學生展示喉嚨模型)我們的聲帶就在這裡。(在模型上指出聲帶的位置)喉嚨四周和裡面有不同的神經線和肌肉，負責控制聲帶。這一對好朋友會一起合作，發出聲音。」

"Now let's guess how long our vocal folds are." (Give students a ruler and have them guess.)

「你們又猜一猜我們的聲帶有多長？」(給學生一把間尺，讓他們猜。)

"The vocal folds grow with age. On average, the vocal folds are 2.5 to 3 mm long for newborn babies, 1 to 1.5 cm long for adult females, and 1.5 to 2 cm long for adult males. The tiny vocal folds are responsible for producing different sounds when we speak. Isn't that amazing?!"

「原來，初生嬰兒的聲帶只有2.5至3毫米長。聲帶會隨著年齡增長而增長，到成年時，女士的聲帶平均長1至1.5厘米，而男士的聲帶平均長1.5至2厘米。我們平日說話的聲音都是靠這兩條小小的聲帶發出的。是否很奇妙呢？」

"The vocal folds are wide open during breathing, looking like the shape of the letter 'V'. When we speak, the vocal folds first come together. They're then set into vibration when air passes through them from the lungs. This is how the voice is made." (Demonstrate vocal fold vibration with both hands. Invite students to imitate.)

「吸氣呼氣的時候，聲帶是打開的，像一個"V"字。(言語治療師用雙手模仿打開的聲帶)說話的時候，聲帶閉緊。空氣從肺部流出時，穿過聲帶，令聲帶振動，從而發出聲音。」(邀請學生用雙手模仿聲帶振動)

"Now, try holding your breath and say 'ah'." (Provide a model for students to imitate.) "As you can see, it's nearly impossible to make any sound when no air is passing through the vocal folds. Now let's breathe in and at the same time say 'ah'." (Provide a model for students to imitate.) "How does it feel? Do you talk like this?" (Let students respond.)

「現在我們來嘗試閉氣時說『呀』。(言語治療師示範並讓學生嘗試)原來閉氣的時候我們幾乎不能發出任何聲音。這次嘗試吸氣的時候說『呀』。(言語治療師示範並讓學生嘗試)覺得怎麼樣？你們平時是這樣說話的嗎？」(讓學生回應)

"You're right! We don't talk like that. It's hard to talk while breathing in. Now, let's try breathing out when saying 'ah'." (Have students try it out with the clinician.) "This time how does it feel? Does it feel much easier?"

「是的。我們平時不會這樣說話。吸氣時說話是很難的。這次嘗試呼氣的時候說『呀』。(學生與言語治療師一起嘗試) 這次感覺又怎麼樣？有容易一點嗎？」

Help the students to realize the strain-strangled voice quality and the feeling when speaking on inhalation. Also, help them to feel the air breathing out during normal phonation.

"Yes! The voice is usually made during exhalation. Respiration provides the energy and power for the voice, like the fuel of a car. Without respiration, the voice cannot be produced."

「是的。我們通常在呼氣時說話。呼吸提供說話的能源，就像汽車裡的汽油一樣。沒有呼吸我們不能發出聲音，就如汽車沒有油不能走動一樣。」

"The vocal folds open and close repeatedly when we talk. When we talk in a high pitch, the vocal folds become stretched and tensed. They become shortened and relaxed when making low-pitched sounds. On average, the vocal folds vibrate 80 to 150 times per second for male speakers and 180 to 240 times for female speakers. Children's vocal fold vibration can be as high as 250 to 300 times per second! The faster they vibrate, the higher the pitch. Therefore, you'll find higher pitches in women and children."

「說話的時候我們的聲帶不斷開合。發高音的時候，我們的聲帶拉長及變得緊張。發低音的時候，聲帶變短和放鬆。男性的聲帶平均一秒振動80至150次，而女性的聲帶平均一秒振動180至240次。大家又猜一猜小朋友的聲帶每秒振動多少次？原來小朋友的聲帶平均每秒可以振動250至300次！聲帶振動頻率愈快，聲音愈高。所以，你會發現女性和小朋友的聲音聽起來比較高音。」

"Let's pretend our hands are the vocal folds. Imagine you're in a library and need to talk softly. (Clap softly for 20 to 30 seconds.) "Now imagine you're yelling on the playground." (Clap loudly for 20 to 30 seconds.) "How do your hands feel?"

「讓我們用手模仿聲帶。想像自己在圖書館裡需要輕聲說話。(輕輕拍掌20至30秒) 現在，想像自己在操場上大叫。(大力拍掌20至30秒) 你們的手覺得怎麼樣？」

Using hand clapping as the analogy for vocal fold vibration, have the students feel the pain when clapping hands vigorously.

"You're right. If we keep clapping hard, our hands get tired or even feel painful. Similarly, when we keep banging the vocal folds hard together, such as yelling and crying, the vocal folds can get tired or even get hurt. Prolonged misuse of the voice can lead to thickening of the vocal folds or abnormal growth such as nodules and polyps. This would disturb vibration of the vocal folds and lead to a hoarse voice."

「是的。若我們不斷用力拍掌，我們的手會感到疲倦，甚至疼痛。聲帶也是一樣，當我們不斷用力拍打它們的時候，如大叫和大哭，我們的聲帶會疲倦，甚至受傷。長期不正確用聲或會導致聲帶變厚，甚至會有異常的生長如『起枕』（即：結節）和瘜肉。這些異常的情況會令聲帶的振動變得不規則，繼而導致聲音沙啞和有氣聲。」

Diagram 2.
Unhealthy vocal folds

圖2.
聲帶生病了

"Let's look at this diagram." (Present **Diagram 2**.) "Do you think the vocal folds are happy or not?" (Have the students share their views.) "Do you know why the vocal folds aren't happy?" (Help the students to realize that the vocal folds are sick.)

「我們看看這張圖，（給學生展示**圖2**）大家覺得聲帶開心嗎？（讓學生回應和表達意見）大家知道聲帶為甚麼會不開心呢？（鼓勵學生猜猜原因，引導他們明白聲帶生病了。）」

"You're right! These vocal folds are unhappy because they're not feeling well. We need to treat them well. Let's learn how to protect the vocal folds."

「對！這幾對聲帶生病了，所以覺得不開心。我們要好好愛護這對好朋友啊。其實保護聲帶好簡單，現在我們來學習怎樣保護聲線，齊齊來做個健康之『聲』！」

Voice rating scale (5 min)

聲線評分表（5分鐘）

Diagram 3.
Voice rating scale

圖3.
聲線評分表

"Let's do an activity. Here I have some recordings of healthy and unhealthy voices. I'd like you to listen to them and rate them on a scale of 10." (Present **Diagram 3**.) "If one sounds very unhealthy, such as severe hoarseness, give a rating of '1.' If the voice sounds very nice and healthy, give a rating of '10.'"

「我們一起來做一個活動。我這裡有多段錄音，一些是健康的聲線，一些是不太健康的聲線。我想請你們聆聽這些錄音，然後給它們評分。（給學生展示**圖3**）若果聲音很不健康，如嚴重聲沙，給它1分；若果聲音很健康，十分清脆響亮，給它10分。」

(Play the voice samples to the students. Ask them to rate the voice quality. Compare and discuss the voice quality ratings. Invite students to explain the reasons for the ratings. Repeat several times.)

（播放錄音，然後請學生互相討論評分，邀請他們說出該評分的理由，重複幾次。若評分相距較大，言語治療師可提供引導。）

For young children who have not developed fine discrimination of voice severity rating, the clinician can focus on training gross discrimination of voice severity (that is, healthy versus dysphonic). Once the children can identify healthy versus dysphonic voices accurately, the clinician can then help them to appreciate fine discrimination of voice severity.

Puppet show: "Star of Healthy Voice" (5 min)

"Let's watch a short video." (Play video)

健康之「聲」布偶戲（5分鐘）

「現在請看一齣布偶戲。」（播放短片）

Vocal hygiene (10 min)

聲線護理（10分鐘）

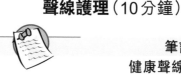

Handout 1.
Quiz on vocal hygiene knowledge

筆記1.
健康聲線知多少？

"After watching the video, fill in the worksheet, and see if you can tell which ones are good vocal habits and which ones are bad vocal habits." (Present **Handout 1**. Allow time for students to fill in the worksheet.)

「看完短片，我們來回答工作紙的問題，分辨哪項是好的和不好的用聲習慣。」（派發**筆記1**，給學生時間完成工作紙。）

"Let's go through the worksheet." (Go through the items one by one with students.)

「讓我們一起核對工作紙的答案。」（言語治療師跟學生逐個項目討論）

In the quiz, the option "not certain" is provided to avoid random guessing. The number of items checked "not certain" can reflect students' level of understanding of the voice care knowledge and hence can be used as an outcome measure.

Answers for the quiz:

Item numbers: 1, 4, 5, 11, 14 [good to the voice]
Item numbers: 2, 3, 6, 7, 8, 9, 10, 12, 13, 15, 16, 17 [harmful to the voice]
The clinician can also discuss with students why and how unhealthy vocal behaviors can harm vocal health (e.g., causing dehydrating effects on the vocal folds [item no. 3, 8], bringing phonotraumatic effects on the vocal folds [item no.: 2, 7, 9, 12, 13, 15, 16], and increasing risks of laryngopharyngeal reflux [item no.: 6, 10, 17]).

Handout 2.	筆記 2.
"Star of Healthy Voice" song	「健康之聲」歌

"Now, let's listen to the song 'Star of Healthy Voice.' The song summarizes the points that are crucial to developing a healthy voice. I want you to pay attention to its lyrics."

「現在讓我們聽一首歌，歌名叫『健康之聲』，這首歌概括了如何保護聲線的要點，我想大家多留意歌詞。」

Diagram 4.	圖 4.
Vocal hygiene	聲帶護理小百科

"This handout lists out the daily habits and vocal habits that can protect the voice."

「這張筆記列出了一些可以保護我們聲線的生活習慣和用聲習慣。」

Conclusion (5 min)　　總結（5分鐘）

Handout 3.	筆記 3.
My healthy voice use agreement	我的護聲約章

"I'd like you to read and sign the healthy voice use agreement." (Present **Handout 3**.) "Promise that you'll drink plenty of water, use your nice and easy voice, and do voice exercises every day, starting today. Be a 'Star of Healthy Voice'!" (Allow time for students to read and sign the agreement.)

「我希望大家由今日開始，一齊努力做個健康之『聲』！現在，請閱讀這份護聲約章（派發**筆記3**），然後在上面簽名，承諾由今天開始多喝水、多用舒服聲說話及做護聲練習。」（讓學生閱讀約章和簽名）

Handout 4.	筆記 4.
Home practice: Session 1	家居用聲練習：第 1 堂

"Good. Here's the home program for this week." (Present **Handout 4**.) I'd like you to record the amount of water you drink each day. Also, rate your voice using the voice-rating scale before you go to bed every night. Check the box for each completed item, and have your parents sign at the end. We'll review your homework next week. Any questions?"

「很好。這是你們今個星期的練習。（派發**筆記4**）我想請你們記錄自己每日喝了多少杯水。另外，請你們每晚睡覺前為自己當天的聲線評分。完成每個項目後，請在家課表上打個"✔"，最後給家長簽名。我下星期會看看你們功課做得如何。有沒有問題？」

Handout 5.
"Star of Healthy Voice" reward chart

筆記 5.
健康之「聲」獎勵表

(Offer stamps on each student's reward chart based on performance in class.)

（言語治療師按學生的課堂表現於學生的獎勵表上蓋印）

"All of you paid attention in class and did a great job today. Each person gets a stamp. Please keep your notes. We'll see who has the most stamps in the last session."

「大家今日很專心上課，每人都得一個蓋印。大家要好好保存筆記，看看最後一堂誰獲得的蓋印最多。」

"I'll see you next week. Bye!"

「我們下星期再見。拜拜。」

Relaxation Exercise, Breathing Exercise, and Humming

Objectives

Students will

1.   present the results of the vocal hygiene home program,

2.   perform relaxation exercise to alleviate excessive body tension,

3.   perform abdominal breathing exercise and practice breathing effectively,

4.   perform humming exercise (/m/) using resonant voice with forward focus and easy phonation, and

5.   evaluate and rate their own voice quality.

Materials

- Worksheets: Handout 6. Activity sheet: Yes-No questions

    Handout 7. Home practice: Session 2

    Handout 8. Recording sheet: Resonant voice practice (nasal /m/)

    Diagram 5. Relaxation exercise

    Diagram 6. Abdominal breathing

    Diagram 7. Forward vs. back tone focus

- Other: Drinking straw 5 to 6 mm in diameter

    Stamp

Session Outline

Introduction (5 min)

"Welcome to the second session. Before we start, let's review the homework from last week. Did you drink enough water? Let me have a look at your self-ratings."

(If the student completed the homework, give him or her a stamp on the reward chart as reinforcement. More stamps can be given according to home practice performance.)

(If the student did not complete the homework, the clinician should discuss with the student the reasons. Give suggestions for improvement.)

"Great! I see that you all made an effort to drink plenty of water last week. This is a very good start. Let's rate your voice today. How would you rate your voice?" (Have the students take turns to rate their voices, using **Diagram 3: Voice Rating Scale** from the previous session.)

"Good. Starting from this week, we'll go through different voice exercises. You'll learn different techniques and will need to practice at home every day."

Relaxation Exercise (10 min)

"First, we'll do stretching exercises to relax the muscles. Do you know stress and body tension can affect the voice? Remember, the larynx is controlled by muscles around the neck. If the muscles are tired or tensed, the voice might sound strained too. Like this." (Demonstrate a strain-strangled voice.) "Therefore, we need to make sure the body is relaxed in order to produce a nice and comfortable voice. Let's do the relaxation exercise together."

引言（5分鐘）

「歡迎來到第二堂。開始之前先看看大家上星期的功課。你們上星期有喝足夠的水嗎？讓我看看你們給自己的評分。」

（若學生有完成功課，在他／她的獎勵表上蓋一個印。言語治療師亦可按學生的家課表現，給予額外蓋印作獎勵。）

（若學生未能完成功課，言語治療師需了解背後的原因，並提供改善建議。）

「很好！大家上星期都有努力喝足夠的水，這是個很好的開始。你們今天會給自己的聲線多少分？」（學生們利用前一堂的**圖3.聲線評分表**輪流為自己的聲線評分）

「很好。從今個星期開始，我們會做一些發聲練習。你們會學習不同的技巧，並需要每天在家裡練習。」

鬆弛運動（10分鐘）

「首先，我們會做鬆弛運動來放鬆身體。你知道壓力和身體繃緊都會影響聲線嗎？要記得，我們的聲帶是靠喉嚨周圍的肌肉控制的。若果肌肉疲勞或繃緊，我們的聲線也會變得緊張，就像這樣。（言語治療師示範繃緊的聲線）因此，若要有舒服的聲線，我們首先要確保身體包括喉嚨是放鬆的。讓我們一同練習這些鬆弛運動。」

The clinician can help students realize how tension affects voice production by asking them to count with raised shoulders and tensed arms. Ask the students to feel the tension in the muscles and the tensed voice quality.

Procedures

步驟

Diagram 5.
Relaxation exercise

圖5.
鬆弛運動

Carry out each step 3 times. Count 5 seconds for contraction and 5 seconds for relaxation. Count silently from 101, 102, 103, to 105.

1. Sit on a chair. Raise the legs from the floor with toes pointing towards self.
2. Clench the fists.
3. Raise the shoulders towards the ears.
4. Have the head down with chin touching the chest.
5. Have the head backward. Tilt as far as possible.
6. Look over the left shoulder.
7. Look over the right shoulder.
8. Massage the larynx (Make a "C" shape with the thumb and the middle finger. Encircle the thyrohyoid space with the fingers and gently pull the thyroid cartilage downward.)

After finishing the above exercises, do a lip trill (also known as bubble lips) with students for 1 to 2 minutes to relax the vocal folds. Vocalize /u/ softly with the lip trill. Glide from a low pitch to a high pitch and then back to the low pitch. (Use analogies such as walking up and down a hill or an airplane taking off and landing, if needed.) Repeat this procedure.

每個動作重複三次,先維持五秒收緊,然後五秒放鬆。心裡數101、102、103直到105。

1. 坐在椅子上,雙腳離地提起,腳板向後拉緊
2. 緊握拳頭
3. 膊頭縮起貼向耳朵
4. 頭向前,下巴貼心口
5. 頭向後,眼望天花板
6. 頭轉向左邊
7. 頭轉向右邊
8. 按摩喉嚨(手呈"C"字形,按著喉嚨兩邊慢慢向下拉。)

完成以上練習後,與學生一起做「振唇練習」一至兩分鐘,用以鬆弛聲帶。振動嘴唇時輕輕發出「烏」聲,由低音慢慢爬到高音再降回低音。(言語治療師可引用上山、落山或飛機升空、降落作比喻。)重複此步驟。

Abdominal Breathing (5 min)

Diagram 6.
Abdominal breathing

"Next, we'll look into how we breathe. Let's put the left palm on the chest and the right palm on the tummy. Take a deep breath gently and slowly. Feel your hand movement." (Invite students to share what they feel and tell/show them your observation.)

"When we breathe in, we should feel the tummy moving outwards. When we breathe out, we should feel the tummy coming back in. The chest and shoulders should not be moving. We call this 'abdominal breathing'. Imagine your tummy is a balloon. Take a deep breath with your nose, and fill up the balloon with air. Do you feel your tummy moving outwards?" (Have students respond.)

"Very good. Now slowly breathe out and feel the movement of your tummy. What do you feel this time?" (Have students respond.)

"Yes! You should feel your tummy come back in when you breathe out."

"Now continue to breathe slowly and feel the movement of your tummy. Count 101, 102, 103 while breathing in, then slowly breathe out. I'll come and check your breathing pattern." (Repeat at least 10 breathing cycles.)

腹式呼吸（5分鐘）

圖6.
腹式呼吸

「接著我們會看看應該怎樣有效地呼吸。把左手放在心口，右手放在肚子上，然後慢慢吸氣，感受呼吸時手的郁動。」（邀請學生分享感受，並告訴他們你的觀察。）

「吸氣時，肚子應該微微脹起；呼氣時，肚子慢慢縮回去，心口和膞頭不應該有郁動，這就是『腹式呼吸』。試幻想肚子是一個氣球。現在用鼻慢慢吸氣，嘗試把氣球充滿。有沒有感受到肚子微微脹起？」（讓學生回應）

「很好。現在慢慢呼氣並感受肚子的郁動。你感覺到甚麼？」（讓學生回應）

「對！呼氣時你應該感受到肚子慢慢縮回去。」

「請繼續慢慢的吸氣呼氣。吸氣的時候請在心裡數101、102、103，然後慢慢呼氣。我會來檢查你們的呼吸。」（重複最少10個呼吸循環）

To promote students' use of abdominal breathing:

1. Use of analogy: The clinician can use an expandable breathing ball as an analogy for abdominal breathing. Ask students to hold the breathing ball in front of the tummy. Expand the ball when breathing in. Contract the ball when breathing out.

2. Visual and tactile cue: Ask students to lie on the back and put a book (or a puppet) on the tummy. Ask students to move the book up and down with the tummy. Note the tummy moving up when breathing in and moving down when breathing out.

3. Begin the breathing cycle with an exhalation: Ask students to breathe out all the air slowly. Let the breath recoil naturally. Note the tummy movement during the recoil.

Establish the resonant voice using a drinking straw (10 min)

(Distribute to each student a drinking straw approximately 0.5 cm in diameter.) "Now, we'll practice a technique called 'the resonant voice' or 'buzzy voice'. This technique encourages easy phonation with minimal tension in the throat. I'd like you to hold the straw with one hand and place it loosely between your lips. Put your other hand at the end of the straw. Now breathe in slowly through the nose and breathe out through the mouth. Do you feel the air flowing out through the straw? Make sure you keep breathing out during the exercise and don't hold your breath. You should feel continuous air flow through the straw." (Check students' airflow with your hand to make sure they are not holding their breath.)

利用飲管幫助建立共鳴聲（10分鐘）

（給每位學生派發一枝直徑約0.5厘米的飲管）「今天我們會學習一個發聲技巧：共鳴聲，或者叫『震震聲』。這個技巧能幫助你輕鬆地發聲。首先請你一隻手拿著飲管，把飲管輕輕放在嘴唇中間。另一隻手則放在飲管的另一端。現在慢慢地用鼻吸氣，然後用口慢慢地呼氣。有沒有感覺到從飲管呼出的空氣？做這個練習時，要保持呼氣，不要閉氣。你應該感覺到空氣不斷從飲管流出。」（言語治療師用手檢查學生是否有呼氣而沒有閉氣）

"Now say /u/ softly on exhalation and tell me what you feel. Again, you should feel air passing out through the straw." (Have students do the exercise several times.) "What do you feel? Do you feel any vibration? Where do you feel the vibration?" (Have students respond. If they cannot tell their feeling, help them by asking: Do you feel the vibration in the back or at the front of the mouth? Do you feel the vibration in your throat, your lips, or your nose?)

「現在請你們呼氣時輕聲講『烏鴉』的『烏』音並拉長，留意感覺到甚麼。記得，發聲時應該感受到從飲管流出的空氣。（讓學生練習幾遍）你們有甚麼感覺？有感覺到振動嗎？哪裡感覺到振動？」（讓學生回應。若學生未能回應，可嘗試進一步引導他們：你感覺振動在喉嚨裡、在嘴唇，還是在鼻子裡？）

Diagram 7.
Forward vs. back tone focus

圖7.
發聲位置圖

"Try to produce a forward resonance. When you phonate, feel the vibration at your lips, your nose, and the back of your front teeth. Your throat should feel relaxed and easy." (Demonstration by the clinician.)

「嘗試把注意力集中在嘴的前方。發聲的時候，感覺嘴唇、鼻和門牙後方的振動。喉嚨應感覺很放鬆。」（言語治療師作正確示範）

"Your voice will sound like this if you have a back tone." (Demonstration by the clinician. Have students explore and feel the difference between forward and back tone focus.)

「若振動集中在喉嚨，聲音會變成這樣。」（言語治療師作反面示範。讓學生摸索和感受前面及後面振動的分別。）

Explore the resonant voice with /m/ (5 min)

探索共鳴聲──「唔～」（5分鐘）

"Now remove the straw. Say /m/ with your lips tightly closed." (Demonstrate.) "This time relax your lips. Have them barely touching each other and say /m/. How does it feel this time? Which one feels easier? Where do you feel the vibration?" (Have students respond.)

「現在請拿掉飲管。嘴唇用力閉緊，然後說『唔～』。（言語治療師示範）這次放鬆嘴唇說『唔～』。這次感覺怎麼樣？哪一個『唔～』感覺放鬆一點？哪裡感覺到振動？」（讓學生回應）

"That's right. We can feel vibratory sensations around the mouth. Sometimes, we may even feel tickling sensations around the teeth."

「對了，用共鳴聲說『唔～』時應該覺得嘴附近有振動，有時候連門牙附近都會覺得痕癢。」

"Good. This time say /m/ with your teeth clenched." (Demonstrate and have students try it out.) Now pretend you're holding a hard-boiled egg in your mouth, with the back of your mouth wide open." (Demonstrate.) "How does it feel this time? Which one is easier?" (Have students respond.)

"Let me hear your nice resonant voice. Open the back of your mouth, relax your lips, and feel the vibration at your nose, lips, and front teeth." (Have students practice.)

「這次嘗試咬緊大牙說『唔～』。(言語治療師示範) 現在在張開嘴巴後方，口裡像含著一隻雞蛋，然後說『唔～』。(言語治療師示範) 這次感覺怎麼樣？哪個感覺較放鬆？」(讓學生回應)

「讓我聽聽你們舒服的共鳴聲。放鬆嘴唇，打開喉嚨，並感受鼻子、嘴唇和門牙的振動。」(讓學生自己練習)

When exploring the resonant voice with young children, the clinician can:

1. Use a visual cue (e.g., fogging up the mirror when phonating) or a tactile cue (e.g., feeling the flow of air with the finger under the nose) to help them exhale air through the nose while humming.
2. Ask the students to place their fingers next to the corner of the clinician's mouth. Ask them to feel the different strengths of vibration when the clinician produces forward versus backward tone production.
3. Use chewing with humming to facilitate the sense of vibration around the lips.

(Give specific feedback on their production based on the following criteria. Provide modeling, tactile cues, and verbal prompts if needed:

1. Easy phonation
2. Relaxed oral and throat muscles, just like you are holding a hard-boiled egg in the mouth
3. Vibratory/buzzing sensations around the lips and front teeth
4. Clear voice)

(Help students evaluate and rate their production.)

(言語治療師為學生的表現給予評語，需要時為學生提供示範、觸覺提示和口頭提示：

1. 輕鬆的發聲
2. 口腔及喉嚨放鬆，嘴裡像含著一隻雞蛋
3. 感受嘴唇和門牙後方有振動
4. 清晰的聲線)

(引導學生為自己的共鳴聲評分)

Activity: Resonant voice 'Yes-No' questions (5 min)

活動：共鳴聲是非題（5分鐘）

Handout 6.
Activity sheet: Yes-No questions

筆記6.
共鳴聲是非題

"Let's play a game. I'm going to ask you some yes-no questions. You can only answer with your good resonant voice 'mm'. If the answer is 'YES', say 'mm-hmm'. If the answer is 'NO', say 'mm-mm'. Let's try one first: 'Do you like watching cartoons?' 'mm-hmm' (yes) or 'mm-mm' (no)?" (Have students respond.)

「我們來玩一個遊戲，我將會問你們一些是非題。你們只可以用共鳴聲『唔～』作答。若果答案是『是』，你們便說"mm-hmm"。若答案是『不是』，你們便說"mm-mm"。我們先試一題：『你們喜歡看卡通片嗎？』"mm-hmm"還是"mm-mm"？」（讓學生回應）

"Very good. Let's do some more." (Students take turns answering the clinician's questions. The clinician can use the yes-no questions in **Handout 6**. Provide feedback on each student's production.)

「很好。我們來多做幾題。（學生輪流回答**筆記6**的是非題。言語治療師為學生的共鳴聲評分。）」

Conclusion (5 min)

總結（5分鐘）

Handout 7.
Home practice: Session 2

筆記7.
家居用聲練習：第2堂

Handout 8.
Recording sheet: Resonant voice practice (nasal /m/)

筆記8.
共鳴聲練習評分表

"Good. Here's the home program for this week. (Present **Handout 7** and **Handout 8**.) Please continue to keep track of the amount of water you drink and rate your voice daily. Also, please do the relaxation exercise, abdominal breathing exercise, and humming exercise twice a day. "

「很好。這是你們今個星期的練習。（派發**筆記7**和**筆記8**）請繼續記錄自己每日喝多少杯水和給自己的聲線評分。另外，請你們每天練習鬆弛運動和腹式呼吸兩遍，此外，大家今日學會了共鳴聲，我想大家每日練習共鳴發聲兩遍。下一堂我們會有更多關於共鳴聲的遊戲。」

(Give stamps on each student's reward chart based on the performance in the session.)

（言語治療師按學生的上課表現於獎勵表上蓋印）

"I'll see you next week. Bye!"

「下星期再見。拜拜！」

Humming with Words

Objectives

Students will

1. present the results of the voice exercise home program,

2. perform relaxation exercise and abdominal breathing as warm-up exercises,

3. produce syllables and words with improved voice quality using resonant voice, and

4. evaluate and rate their own voice quality.

Materials

*   Worksheets: Handout 9. Practice stimuli: Single-syllable word list

    Handout 10. Practice stimuli: Two-syllable word list

    Handout 11. Home practice: Session 3

    Handout 12. Recording sheet: Resonant voice practice (single-syllable words)

    Handout 13. Recording sheet: Resonant voice practice (two-syllable words)

    Diagram 8. Word cards (for sentence composition game)

*   Other: Stamp

    Turn-taking games (e.g., Connect 4, Don't Break the Ice)

Session Outline

Introduction (5 min)

"Welcome to the third session. Let's review the homework from last week. How did your home program go last week?" (If students completed the home program, reward them with a stamp. Give out more stamps if they show good progress.)

(Ask the students to count the number of stamps received so far as motivation.)

"Great. Now let's rate your voice today." (Have each student rate his/her voice using **Diagram 3: Voice rating scale.**)

Relaxation and breathing exercises (5 min)

"Let's begin our session with relaxation exercise." (Lead the relaxation exercise following the procedures covered in Session Two. Observe whether the students perform the exercise properly. Provide feedback/reminders when needed.)

"Good. Let's do the breathing exercise." (Lead the breathing exercise. Breathe in and breathe out slowly for 1 minute. Observe whether the students use abdominal breathing. Provide modeling and visual/verbal/tactile prompts if needed.)

Resonant voice practice: /m/ and Yes-No questions (5 min)

"Last week, we learned how to make the resonant voice (or buzzy voice). Let's review."

"Remember where we should feel the vibration when we hum?" (Have students respond. Make use of **Diagram 7: Forward vs. back tone focus** from the previous session, if needed.)

引言（5分鐘）

「歡迎來到第三堂。開始之前先看看你們上星期的家課做得如何。對於上星期的家課，你們有任何問題或有甚麼想分享？」（若學生有完成功課，在他/她的獎勵表上蓋一個印，表現良好的學生可獲得更多蓋印。）

（請學生匯報到目前為止所獲得蓋印的數量）

「很好。現在我想請你們為今天的聲線評分。」（學生利用**圖3. 聲線評分表**評分）

鬆弛運動和腹式呼吸練習（5分鐘）

「首先，我們會一起做鬆弛運動。」（言語治療師帶領鬆弛運動，亦可邀請學生作小助手帶領。運動步驟和第二堂一樣。言語治療師觀察學生的表現，看看節奏是否適中？有否充份感受收緊和放鬆？並在需要時給予反饋及提醒。）

「接著，我們會做呼吸練習。」（言語治療師或小助手帶領練習。慢慢吸氣呼氣一分鐘。觀察學生是否運用腹式呼吸。需要時給予學生示範和視覺/口頭/觸覺提示。）

共鳴聲練習──「唔～」和是非題（5分鐘）

「上星期我們學會了如何發出共鳴聲（或『震震聲』）。讓我們複習一遍。」

「大家還記得發聲時，應該在哪裡感到振動呢？」（讓學生回應，如有需要，可使用前一堂的**圖7. 發聲位置圖**。）

"That's right. Let's make a back tone focus together with /m/ (negative practice). Now move it forward to the front of your mouth. Pretend you're holding a hard-boiled egg in your mouth, and keep your lips relaxed. Your throat should feel relaxed and comfortable." (Have students tell you where they feel the vibrations and if the voice feels comfortable. Provide modelling and visual/verbal/tactile prompts if needed. Practice shifting the voice from front to back and back to front several times. Do this activity for several minutes.)

「對了。試用喉嚨聲説『唔～』。(錯誤示範) 現在把振動向前移。想像嘴裡含著一隻雞蛋，嘴唇放鬆，喉嚨也放鬆。」(引導學生告訴你他們感覺到振動嗎？哪裡感覺到振動？喉嚨舒服嗎？需要時給學生提供示範或視覺／口頭／觸覺提示。練習把聲音從前面向後移，再由後面向前移。重複幾次。練習數分鐘。)

"Good. Let's answer some Yes-No questions with your nice and easy voice, 'mm-hmm' or 'mm-mm', like last week." (Students take turns to answer yes-no questions. Practice for 1 to 2 minutes.)

「很好。現在用共鳴聲 (『震震聲』) 回答一些問題：" mm-hmm "或" mm-mm "。」(學生輪流回答問題 1-2 分鐘)

If the student demonstrates difficulty in achieving a good hum due to:

1. abrupt onset of humming, facilitate gentle onset using sighing by asking the student to sigh and then blend it into humming (/h . . . m/).
2. tight lips during humming, loosen the lips using lip trill. Ask the student to do a lip trill and blend it into humming (lip trill . . . /m/).
3. lack of oral resonance, increase frontal oral resonance by widening oropharyngeal space using chewing. Ask the student to produce humming while chewing. This exercise will also allow the student to feel the buzzy sensation around the lips and the nose more easily during phonation.

Resonant voice practice: single-syllable word (10 min)

共鳴聲練習——單字 (10 分鐘)

"This week we'll practice saying single and multi-syllable words using resonant voice."

「今個星期我們會練習用共鳴聲説單字和詞語。」

Handout 9.
Practice stimuli: Single-syllable word list

筆記 9.
共鳴聲：單字表

"We begin with our nice 'mmm' sound. Slowly proceed and blend into the single-syllable word." (Demonstrate the first item on the word list: /m/ + /a/.)

(Explain and demonstrate the criteria for good production. Use negative practice when necessary.)

"Do you know how to judge the production? A good production should lead to:

1. easy phonation,
2. relaxed oral and throat muscles, just like holding an egg in your mouth,
3. vibratory/buzzing sensations felt around lips and front teeth,
4. steady phonation with hum and words well-linked, and
5. a clear voice."

"Let's practice /m/ + /a/ together 3 times." (Go through the single-syllable words one by one. Practice each word 3 times. The clinician provides a model for the students to imitate. Invite parents to try it out too.)

"How would you rate your production?" (Students rate their production. The clinician rates students' production as well. Compare the ratings.)

(Provide specific feedback on the production.) "Excellent! I noted your relaxed throat when saying /m/ + /a/. Also, you demonstrated steady phonation and forward resonance. I'd give you a score of 8. You can get a higher score of 9 if you can say /m/ + /a/ with a happy and relaxed face."

「首先，我們用舒服聲説『唔～』，然後慢慢連接後面的單字。」(言語治療師示範「唔……呀」)

(説明並示範良好發聲的標準，有需要時可使用錯誤示範。)

「你知道如何判斷好的發聲嗎？良好的發聲需要：

1. 輕鬆的發聲
2. 放鬆口腔及喉嚨，嘴裡像含著一隻雞蛋
3. 感受嘴唇和門牙後方有振動
4. 哼聲與字之間串聯起來，像好朋友般大家手牽手
5. 清晰的聲線」

「現在你們自己練習『唔＋呀』三次。」(順次序逐個單字練習，每個字練習三次。言語治療師先示範。邀請家長一起練習。)

「你們會給自己多少分？」(學生給自己的表現評分，言語治療師也給學生評分，比較大家評分的差距。)

(給學生具體的反饋)「非常好！我聽到你説『唔＋呀』時喉嚨有放鬆，而且『唔』和『呀』字有串聯起來，聲線位置在口前方，我會給你8分，如果嘴巴能夠再加以放鬆就更加理想，便可以有9分。」

Resonant voice practice: Two-syllable word (10 min)

共鳴聲練習——雙字詞語（10分鐘）

<table>
<tr><td>Handout 10.
Practice stimuli: Two-syllable word list</td><td>筆記10.
共鳴聲：雙字詞語表</td></tr>
</table>

"Good. Let's move one level up. This time we'll practice saying some two-syllable words. Let's practice the first three words together." (Provide a model for students and parents to imitate.)

「很好。練習完單字，這次我們會練習一些詞語。讓我們一起練習首三個詞語。」（言語治療師示範，學生和家長重複練習。）

"Now I'm going to pair you up with your mom/dad (whoever brought the student to the session). You'll take turns reading out the rest of the words and rate each other's production." (Go to each group and give feedback to students and parents.)

「接下來的詞語，我會請你和媽媽／爸爸（照顧者）一起練習。請你們輪流讀出餘下的詞語，然後互相評分。」（言語治療師到每組視察，並對各人的表現給予評價。）

> Rationale for involving caregivers in the session:
> 1. Provide students with intrinsic motivation when rating the caregiver's voice.
> 2. Provide opportunities to rate others' voices. This can improve students' perceptual rating skills and self-awareness.
> 3. Ensure parents/caregivers can provide good models for their children and provide accurate feedback on their children's performance at home.

Turn-taking game (8 min)

輪流遊戲（8分鐘）

(Materials: Turn-taking games such as "Connect 4" and "Don't Break the Ice")

（教材：輪流遊戲如"Connect 4"和"Don't Break the Ice"）

<table>
<tr><td>Diagram 8.
Word cards</td><td>圖8.
詞語遊戲卡</td></tr>
</table>

"Lastly, we will play a game together. Pick a card and read aloud the word using your nice resonant voice. You'll receive a token for a nice production."

「最後我們會玩輪流遊戲。先抽一張字卡，若你能用漂亮的共鳴聲讀出抽到的詞語，便可得到一顆棋子。」

(Pick a turn-taking game that is age-appropriate and motivating to students. Decide the number of words said on each turn. Provide students with modeling or visual/verbal/tactile prompts if needed to help them achieve a good resonant voice.)

（言語治療師按照學生的年紀及喜好挑選遊戲。言語治療師能決定學生每次說多少個詞語。玩遊戲時，多鼓勵學生對自己的共鳴聲評分，言語治療師亦要運用臨床判斷，需要時給學生提供示範或視覺／口頭／觸覺提示，以幫助學生掌握共鳴聲的運用。）

Conclusion (2 min)

Handout 11.
Home practice: Session 3

Handout 12.
Recording sheet: Resonant voice practice
(single-syllable words)

Handout 13.
Recording sheet: Resonant voice practice
(two syllable words)

總結（2分鐘）

筆記11.
家居用聲練習：第3堂

筆記12.
共鳴聲練習評分表（單字）

筆記13.
共鳴聲練習評分表（詞語）

"This week, continue to record your water intake, do relaxation exercise and abdominal breathing exercise twice per day, and rate your voice daily. Also, I have a worksheet for you and your parent/caregiver to complete at home." (Present **Handouts 12 and 13**.) "Please practice with your parents and rate each other's voice, like we did in the session today. Write down your parent's score on the worksheet. Your parent does the same. Please practice reading the words, preferably twice and at least once a day."

(Offer stamps on the reward chart based on each student's performance.)

"That's all for today. I'll see you all next week."

「今個星期請你們繼續記錄自己的喝水數量，每天做鬆弛運動和腹式呼吸練習兩次，並為自己的聲線評分。另外，我有一張工作紙給你和家長／照顧者在家完成。〔派發共鳴聲練習工作紙，一張供**單字**（筆記**12**），一張供**詞語**（筆記**13**）用〕，請與家長一起練習，就像剛才上課時做的練習一樣，互相評分，把評分寫在工作紙上。請每天在家練習兩次但可最少一次。」

（言語治療師按學生的上課表現於學生的獎勵表上蓋印）

「好，今堂結束了，下星期再見。」

Humming with Phrases and Sentences

Objectives

Students will

1. present the results of the voice exercise home program,

2. perform relaxation exercise and abdominal breathing as warm-up exercises,

3. produce phrases and sentences with improved voice quality using resonant voice, and

4. evaluate and rate their own voice quality.

Materials

- Worksheets: Handout 14. Practice stimuli: Sentence list

  Handout 15. Activity sheet: Sentence composition game

  Handout 16. Home practice: Session 4

  Handout 17. Recording sheet: Resonant voice practice (sentences)

  Diagram 8. Word cards (for sentence composition game)

- Other: Timer

  Stamp

Session Outline

Introduction (5 min)

"Welcome to session four. Let's review the homework for last week. How did your home program go last week?" (If the student completed his/her home program, reward him/her with a stamp.)

"Great. Now let's rate your voice today." (Have each student rate his/her voice using **Diagram 3: Voice rating scale**.)

Relaxation and breathing exercises (5 min)

"Let's start with relaxation exercise." (Invite a student to lead the relaxation exercise.)

"Next, let's practice abdominal breathing." (Invite another student to lead the practice.)

Resonant voice practice: nasal /m/, single- and two-syllable words (10 min)

"Now let's practice the nice resonant voice. Remember to relax your lips and open the back of your mouth, like holding a hard-boiled egg in your mouth. Feel the vibration at the front of your mouth."

(Demonstrate the /m/ sound produced with back resonance. Slowly move the sound to the front of the mouth with forward resonance.)

"Now let me hear your nice resonant voice /m/." (Give specific feedback on students' production.)

"Good. Now let's read aloud some words using forward resonance." (Materials: Word cards)

引言（5分鐘）

「歡迎來到第四堂。開始之前先看看你們上星期的家課做得如何。對於上星期的家課，你們有沒有問題或有甚麼想分享？」（若學生有完成功課，在他／她的獎勵表上蓋一個印。）

「很好。現在我想請你們為今天的聲線評分。」（學生利用**圖3. 聲線評分表**評分）

鬆弛運動和腹式呼吸練習（5分鐘）

「我們先做鬆弛運動。」（言語治療師邀請學生帶領做鬆弛運動）

「接著，我們做呼吸練習。」（言語治療師邀請另一位學生帶領做練習）

共鳴聲練習──「唔～」，單字／詞語（10分鐘）

「現在我們練習共鳴聲『唔～』。記得放鬆嘴唇，嘴巴後方張開，像含著一隻雞蛋。感受嘴巴前方的振動。」

（言語治療師先示範喉嚨聲，然後慢慢把聲音向前移。）

「現在讓我聽聽你們很好聽的共鳴聲。」（言語治療師給予具體的反饋）

「好，現在讓我們用共鳴聲讀詞語。」
（材料：詞語卡）

(Have students practice for 1 to 2 minutes. Provide specific feedback on students' production.)

（讓學生自行練習。言語治療師在旁聆聽，並給予反饋。練習一至兩分鐘。）

Resonant voice practice: Sentence (10 min)

共鳴聲練習──句子（10分鐘）

Handout 14.
Practice stimuli: Sentence list

筆記14.
共鳴聲：句子

"Well done, everyone. Today, we'll practice reading sentences aloud using a resonant voice."

「大家的共鳴聲練習做得很好，今堂我們將會練習用共鳴聲讀句子。」

(Read aloud the sentences one by one. Give specific feedback on students' production. Encourage students to rate their own performance.)

（跟著筆記上的句子逐一練習，言語治療師給予具體的反饋，並鼓勵學生為自己的共鳴聲評分。）

> If the student has difficulty in maintaining good forward resonance throughout the sentence, decrease the step by adding words one by one. For example:
> 唔～～媽
> 唔～～媽媽
> 唔～～媽媽摸
> 唔～～媽媽摸貓

(Gradually fade the use of the hum as a prompt in saying the sentences while maintaining the buzz sensation or forward resonance.) "Let's read aloud the sentences again without the /m/ onset." (Clinician demonstrates.)

（逐漸減去讀句子時使用「唔」音開始，但句子仍要保持良好的共鳴。）「我們再練習用共鳴聲讀這些句子，我想大家將『唔』音在心裡默唸，然後讀出句子。」（言語治療師示範）

"Remember, we need to maintain good forward resonance even though we don't begin the sentence with humming. Who can tell us the key features of good forward resonance? Yes, a good production should lead to:

1. easy phonation,
2. relaxed oral and throat muscles, just like holding an egg in your mouth,
3. vibratory sensations felt around lips and front teeth,
4. steady phonation with the words well-linked together, and
5. a clear voice."

「要緊記，雖然沒有『唔』作句子起首，我們仍要保持良好的共鳴，誰可以告訴大家，良好的共鳴是怎樣的呢？對，良好的共鳴需要：

1. 輕鬆的發聲
2. 放鬆口腔及喉嚨，嘴裡像含著一隻雞蛋
3. 感受嘴唇和門牙後方有振動
4. 字與字之間串聯起來，像好朋友般大家手牽手
5. 清晰的聲線」

(The clinician can also choose sentences with consonant /m/ as the onset of the first word. Lengthen the consonant /m/ to promote students' awareness of forward resonance (buzzy sensation) when reading aloud.)

（言語治療師亦可選取起首為聲母/m/的句子，閱讀時稍為拉長/m/音，以協助維持共鳴腔。）

Game: Sentence composition challenge (10 min)

"Let's have a competition."

Materials: Word cards, writing sheet, timer

遊戲：共鳴聲作句大挑戰（10分鐘）

「我們來個比賽。」

材料：詞語卡，作句紙，計時器

Handout 15.
Activity sheet: Sentence composition game

筆記15.
共鳴聲作句大挑戰

(Students will be asked to draw three word cards. They have to compose as many sentences as they can in 3 minutes, using the words drawn. When the time is up, students will read aloud their sentences using their nice resonant voice. Students will be scored based on the number of sentences composed and the quality of their hums.)

（學生需在限時三分鐘內利用言語治療師給予的詞語卡作句。限時過後，學生們輪流用共鳴聲讀出所作的句子。言語治療師將按照學生作句的數量和發聲的質素評分，以決定給予多少個印章。）

The clinician/parent can assist with writing out the sentences if students do not know how to write particular words. Try using daily phrases to promote generalization.

Conclusion (5 min)

Handout 16. Home Practice: Session 4	
Handout 17. Recording sheet: Resonant voice practice (sentences)	

"This week, continue to record your water intake, do relaxation and breathing exercises twice a day, and rate your voice every day." (Present **Handouts 16 and 17**.) "Also, practice reading aloud all the words and sentences we learned."

(Lastly, the clinician offer stamps on each student's reward chart based on class performance.)

"That's all for today. I'll see you all next week."

總結（5分鐘）

筆記16. 家居用聲練習：第4堂	
筆記17. 共鳴聲練習評分表（句子）	

「很好。這是你們今個星期的練習。（派發**筆記16和筆記17**）請繼續記錄自己每日的喝水數量，做鬆弛運動和腹式呼吸練習，並給自己的聲線評分。另外，請你們練習學過的句子。」

（最後，言語治療師按學生的上課表現於學生的獎勵表上蓋印。）

「我們下星期再見。」

Humming with Passages and Loudness Control

Objectives

Students will

1. present the results of the voice exercise home program,

2. perform relaxation exercise and abdominal breathing as warm-up exercises,

3. read aloud short passages with improved voice quality using resonant voice,

4. demonstrate precise control of vocal loudness, and

5. evaluate and rate their own voice quality.

Materials

-   Worksheets: Handout 18. Practice stimuli: Passage and voice projection

    Handout 19. Activity sheet: Change in vocal loudness

    Handout 20. Home Practice: Session 5

-   Other: Timer

    Stamp

    Device with computer applications for real-time loudness display

Session Outline

Introduction (5 min)

"Welcome! It's already the fifth session. Did you do your home exercise last week?" (The clinician checks students' home exercise chart. If the student completed his/her home program, reward him/her with a stamp.)

引言（5分鐘）

「歡迎！來到第五堂了。你們有完成家課嗎？」（言語治療師核對學生的家居練習表。若學生有完成家課，在他／她的獎勵表上蓋一個印。）

Relaxation and breathing exercises (5 min)

"Let's start with the relaxation exercise."

"Next, let's practice abdominal breathing."

鬆弛運動和腹式呼吸練習（5分鐘）

「我們先做鬆弛運動。」

「接著，我們會做呼吸練習。」

Resonant voice practice: Nasal /m/ (5 min)

(Students hum with forward focus as warm-up.)

共鳴聲練習——「唔～」（5分鐘）

（學生用共鳴聲哼「唔～」作熱身）

Resonant voice practice: Short passage (10 min)

共鳴聲練習——短文（10分鐘）

Handout 18.
Practice stimuli: Passage and voice projection

筆記18.
共鳴聲練習＋聲線放送

"Good. Now we'll practice reading aloud a passage with forward resonance. We'll also practice effective voice projection so that your voice can reach further."

"Here's a short passage. First, I'd like you to read it aloud in one single breath. Tell me how you feel and how your voice sounds afterwards." (Students can also choose any passage of their own.)

"Yes, the voice sounds tight. This time, I want you to read the passage again. Add a 'hum' at the beginning of each sentence. Take a breath for each sentence."

「好，現在我們來練習如何在朗讀課文時應用共鳴聲。我們還會練習如何有效地把聲線傳送得更遠。」

「這裡有一篇短文。首先，我請大家嘗試一口氣把整篇文章朗讀出來。告訴我，你們感覺如何？你們覺得自己的聲音怎樣？」（學生亦可自選課文）

「對啊，聲音聽起來很繃緊，喉嚨會較疲倦。現在再朗讀課文一遍，請你們在每句句子的開端先輕輕吸氣並加上『唔～』音。」

(The clinician demonstrates passage reading using resonant voice and talks about appropriate speech rate and use of pauses. Students then practice reading aloud the short passage on their own.)

"Excellent! Let's read the passage again but without the hum. Maintain good forward resonance while reading." (Give specific feedback to individual students.)

（言語治療師先示範用共鳴聲朗讀短文，教導正確語速和適當停頓。接著，學生自己練習朗讀課文。）

「非常好，我們再讀文章而不用『唔～』音幫助，看看大家能否保持良好的共鳴腔。」（給予學生具體的反饋）

Resonance voice: Loudness control (15 min)

音量控制練習（15分鐘）

Handout 19.
Activity sheet: Change in vocal loudness

筆記19.
音量變化練習

"In this session we'll also practice control of vocal loudness. Do you know why we need to practice the use of different vocal loudness? We use different vocal loudness in different environments. For example, we speak softly in quiet libraries. We raise the voice when we need to speak on a noisy street."

「今堂我們會練習如何控制聲量。你們知道為甚麼我們需要練習使用不同的聲量嗎？在日常生活中，我們會因應需要而用不同聲量說話，例如：在圖書館要輕聲說話；在嘈雜的環境要提高聲量。」

"First, practice saying /m/ . . . (single-syllable word) using your comfortable voice. Then, practice saying it from soft to loud." (The clinician can use mobile phone apps that display real-time vocal loudness as biofeedback.) "Next, practice saying it first from soft to loud, then from loud to soft." (Make sure that students are using abdominal breathing while practicing.)

「先練習用舒服聲說『唔＋（單字）』。然後練習由細聲變大聲。（練習時可用量度音量的手機應用程式作視覺反饋）跟著再練習由細聲變大聲再變細聲。」（練習時，注意學生是否有用腹式呼吸。）

"Good. Let's have someone be the conductor to lead the others to a change in loudness."

「好，現在請一位同學做指揮，指示其他人的聲量變化。」

> When practicing loudness control, children may easily increase loudness with vocal effort, which is not ideal. The clinician should clarify and remind students to raise their vocal loudness using a well-projected voice. Project the voice efficiently with good breath support, good oral resonance, and sufficiently opened mouth during speech.

Conclusion (5 min)

Handout 20.
Home Practice: Session 5

"Here's the home program for this week." (Present **Handout 20.**) "Please continue to do what you've been doing with the water intake record and the vocal exercises. Also, I'd like you to practice talking to your parents using your nice resonant voice at home. Try to practice talking with your family members in noisy backgrounds using a well-projected voice. Any questions?"

"I'll see you next week. Bye!"

總結（5分鐘）

筆記20.
家居用聲練習：第5堂

「這是你們今個星期的練習。（派發**筆記20**）請你們繼續記錄每日的喝水數量和做練習。另外，請你們在家練習用共鳴聲與家人對話，並嘗試練習在嘈吵的地方運用共鳴聲投放聲線。大家有沒有問題？」

「我們下星期再見。拜拜！」

Voice Projection and Conclusion

Objectives

Students will

1. present the results of the voice exercise home program,

2. perform relaxation exercise and abdominal breathing as warm-up exercises,

3. maintain use of forward resonance in daily conversations,

4. evaluate and rate their own voice quality, and

5. formulate a plan to maintain a healthy voice.

Materials

- Worksheets: Handout 21. Home practice: Session 6
  Handout 22. My voice protection plan

- Other: Timer
  Stamp

Session Outline

Introduction (5 min)

"Welcome all! This is our last session. Let's check the homework from last week. Did you practice using your nice resonant voice at home?" (Reward students with a stamp if homework is completed. Give more stamps for good performance.)

引言（5分鐘）

「來到最後一堂了。讓我看看你們上星期的練習。你們有沒有練習用響亮的共鳴聲說話？」（檢查學生的家居練習表。若學生有完成功課，在他／她的獎勵表上蓋一個印。）

Relaxation and breathing exercise (5 min)

"Let's start with the relaxation exercise."

"Next, let's practice abdominal breathing."

鬆弛運動和腹式呼吸練習（5分鐘）

「我們先做鬆弛運動。」

「接著，我們會做呼吸練習。」

Guessing game (20 min)

Materials: Guessing game stimuli (from stimulus cards), timer

Procedures:
1. Students take turns to be the guesser or the describer.
2. Guesser and describer stand on opposite ends of the room, facing each other. Keep approximately 2 m apart.
3. The clinician stands behind the guesser, facing the describer. The clinician holds up picture stimuli for the describer to describe. The guesser guesses what the picture is about.
4. Each round lasts for 3 minutes. The clinician can assist the describer when needed.
5. Lastly, see how many pictures the guesser is able to guess.

* Students may get excited while playing. The clinician should pay attention to whether the students use their best voice possible. Give verbal reminders when needed.

遊戲：猜一猜（20分鐘）

材料：猜一猜遊戲圖片，計時器

步驟：
1. 一位學生負責描述，另一位學生負責猜。
2. 負責描述和猜的同學會面對面站在房間的兩邊，相距約兩米。
3. 言語治療師會站在負責猜的同學後面，面向負責描述的同學，同時會舉起圖片給描述者形容。負責猜的同學要猜圖片是甚麼。
4. 每個回合三分鐘。如有需要，言語治療師可協助描述者形容圖片。
5. 最後，看看負責猜的同學猜中多少圖片。

* 遊戲時，言語治療師會留意描述者的發聲方法，看看學生會否因玩至忘形而忘記保持共鳴聲，有需要時給予口頭提示。

The clinician can increase the level of difficulty to further promote effective voice projection. This can be done either by increasing the distance between students or by increasing the background ambient noise level (e.g., the clinician can record the noise on the playground during school recess and present the audio file during the game). Remind students of the use of the resonance voice and nice voice projection.

Formulate own therapy plan (10 min)

聲線保護計劃（10分鐘）

Handout 21.
Home practice: Session 6

筆記21.
家居用聲練習：第6堂

"Here's the home program for this week." (Present **Handout 21**.)

「這是你們今個星期的練習。（派發**筆記21**）」

Handout 22.
My voice protection plan

筆記22.
我的聲線保護計劃

"Lastly, I would like each of you to formulate your own voice protection plan to remind yourself of what you can do to restore your voice if you get sick one day, or experience a sore throat or voice loss." (Help the students to brainstorm suggestions.)

「最後，我想大家訂立一套聲線保護計劃，用作提醒自己日後生病了，或遇到喉嚨痛、聲沙或失聲等問題，你們會做甚麼去讓聲音早日復原。」（言語治療師可給予建議）

Conclusion (5 min)

總結（5分鐘）

"Congratulations! You've successfully completed the voice program. I hope that you'll keep protecting and using your nice voice. Be a 'Star of Healthy Voice'!"

「恭喜你！你們已經成功完成了整個治療課程。我希望你們能繼續保護和運用你們的聲線，做個『健康之聲』！」

Handouts and Diagrams

筆記 1. 健康聲線知多少？

你認為以下各項因素，哪一項有助保護聲線，哪一項會損害聲線？請在適當的空格劃上 "✓"。

		有助保護聲線 ✓	會損害聲線 ✗	不清楚 ?
1.	有足夠睡眠			
2.	長期咳嗽			
3.	用口呼吸			
4.	多飲水			
5.	保持良好的姿勢			
6.	吸煙			
7.	放縱地大笑／大哭			
8.	飲可樂、咖啡、茶			
9.	說話急速			
10.	在空氣混濁的地方交談			
11.	多做伸展運動			
12.	清喉嚨			
13.	扮汽車引擎聲、怪獸聲			
14.	保持心境開朗			
15.	尖叫			
16.	以氣音不出聲（即：秘密聲）說話			
17.	吃刺激性（甜、酸、辣）食物			

© Ma 2023. *Voice Therapy for Children: An Instructional Manual.*

筆記 2.「健康之聲」歌

C 大調　　　曲/詞: Sunny Wong

健康之聲　健康之聲

唱歌說話　要靠那聲帶發聲

平日說話要慢　輕聲不尖叫

要喝水　多些休息　多放鬆

能學會護理聲音　別人可細聽

用那腹式呼吸　代替胸式呼吸

肚子脹又縮　夠氣不需過急

然後坐下再拉筋 按摩喉嚨

用嘆聲哼聲　將聲音放鬆

回復美妙動聽聲音　能做到

© Ma 2023. *Voice Therapy for Children: An Instructional Manual.*

筆記 3. 我的護聲約章

我＿＿＿＿＿＿＿＿＿＿＿＿承諾由今天開始：

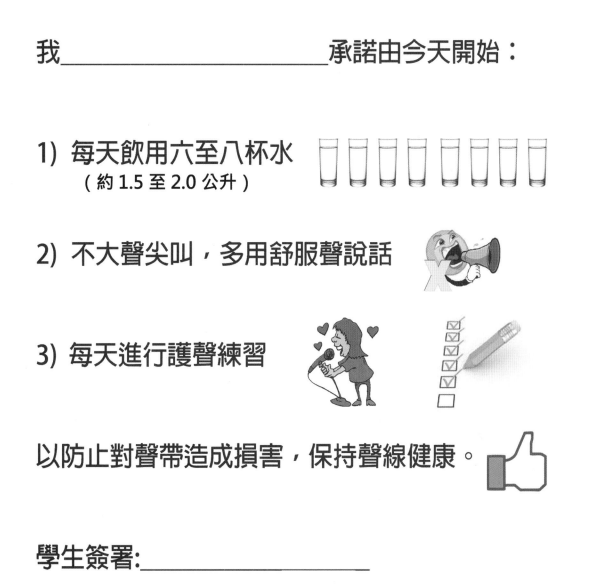

1) 每天飲用六至八杯水
   （約 1.5 至 2.0 公升）

2) 不大聲尖叫，多用舒服聲說話

3) 每天進行護聲練習

以防止對聲帶造成損害，保持聲線健康。

學生簽署:＿＿＿＿＿＿＿＿＿＿＿

© Ma 2023. *Voice Therapy for Children: An Instructional Manual.*

筆記 4. 家居用聲練習：第 1 堂

完成每個練習項目後，於空格填上 "✓"，並給家長簽名。

家居練習	日期					
1.　每天喝六至八杯水（約 1.5 至 2.0 公升）						
2.　注意聲線護理（輕聲說話不大聲尖叫，少吃刺激性食物等）						
3.　為自己的聲線評分（請把分數寫在空格內）　1 2 3 4 5 6 7 8 9 10						
家長簽名						

© Ma 2023. *Voice Therapy for Children: An Instructional Manual.*

筆記 5. 健康之「聲」獎勵表

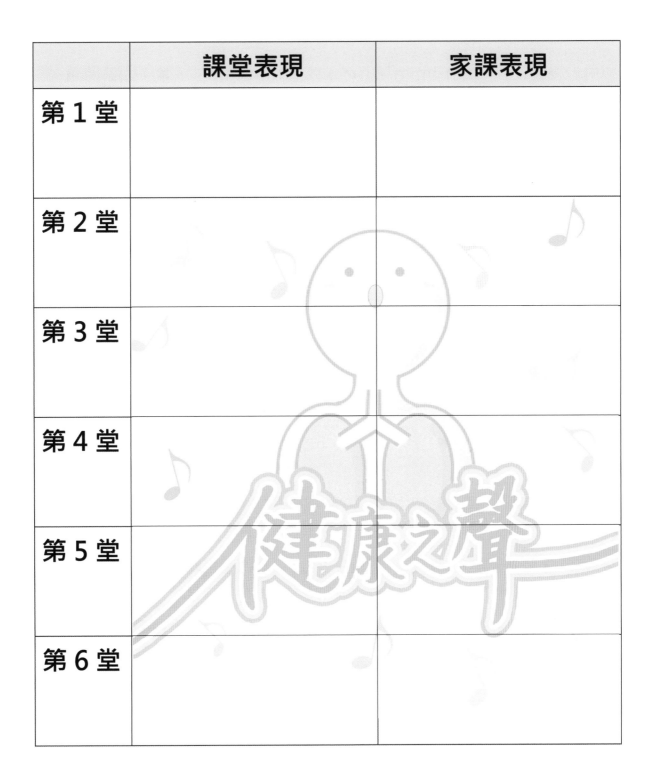

	課堂表現	家課表現
第 1 堂		
第 2 堂		
第 3 堂		
第 4 堂		
第 5 堂		
第 6 堂		

© Ma 2023. *Voice Therapy for Children: An Instructional Manual.*

筆記 6. 共鳴聲是非題

利用「震震聲」"mm-hmm"（✔）或 "mm-mm"（✘）回答問題

數學
1. 1+1=2 (✔)
2. 3+2=6 (✘)
3. 5+5=10 (✔)
4. 11−3=8 (✔)
5. 15−3=11 (✘)
6. 10+20=40 (✘)
7. 1+2+3=6 (✔)
8. 4+3+2=10 (✘)
9. 5+6+7=18 (✔)
10. 8+9−10=6 (✘)

日常生活
1. 紅燈時我們應該過馬路嗎？(✘)
2. 上課時可以玩電話嗎？(✘)
3. 抽煙對身體有益。(✘)
4. 我們應該多吃蔬菜和水果。(✔)
5. 吃飯前應洗手。(✔)
6. 睡覺前要刷牙。(✔)

個人（沒有預設答案）
1. 你喜歡上學嗎？
2. 你喜歡英文課嗎？
3. 你喜歡數學課嗎？
4. 你喜歡吃巧克力嗎？
5. 你喜歡吃榴槤嗎？
6. 你喜歡唱歌嗎？
7. 你喜歡畫畫嗎？
8. 你會游泳嗎？
9. 你喜歡自己的聲線嗎？
10. 你愛你的爸爸媽媽嗎？

© Ma 2023. *Voice Therapy for Children: An Instructional Manual.*

筆記 7. 家居用聲練習：第 2 堂

完成每個練習項目後，於空格填上 "✓"，並給家長簽名。

家居練習	日期					
1. 每天喝六至八杯水 （約 1.5 至 2.0 公升）						
2. 注意聲線護理 （輕聲說話不大聲尖叫，少吃刺激性食物等）						
3. 鬆弛運動和腹式呼吸 （每天練習兩遍）						
4. 共鳴聲練習 （每天練習兩遍，每遍練習共鳴聲 10 次，並把分數填在筆記 8 內）						
5. 為自己的聲線評分 （請把分數寫在空格內） 1 2 3 4 5 6 7 8 9 10						
家長簽名						

© Ma 2023. *Voice Therapy for Children: An Instructional Manual.*

筆記 8. 共鳴聲練習評分表

學生和家長輪流練習共鳴聲「唔」，並互相為對方評分：

評分準則：　　1. 輕鬆的發聲
　　　　　　　2. 放鬆口腔及喉嚨
　　　　　　　3. 感受嘴唇和門牙後方的振動
　　　　　　　4. 清晰的聲線

日期	評分	次數									
		1	2	3	4	5	6	7	8	9	10
	學生										
	家長										
	學生										
	家長										
	學生										
	家長										
	學生										
	家長										
	學生										
	家長										
	學生										
	家長										

© Ma 2023. *Voice Therapy for Children: An Instructional Manual.*

筆記 9. 共鳴聲：單字表

1. 唔 ~

2. 唔 → 媽

3. 唔 → 咩

4. 唔 → 咪

5. 唔 → 麼

6. 唔 → 嗚

7. 唔 → 貓

8. 唔 → 芒

9. 唔 → 檬

10. 唔 → 麵

發共鳴聲時，要留意：

1. 發聲是否輕鬆

2. 口腔及喉嚨是否放鬆

3. 感受嘴唇和門牙後方的振動

4. 哼聲與字之間有否串聯起來

5. 聲線的清晰度

© Ma 2023. *Voice Therapy for Children: An Instructional Manual.*

筆記 10. 共鳴聲：雙字詞語表

1. 唔 ~

2. 唔 → 媽媽

3. 唔 → 芒果

4. 唔 → 貓咪

5. 唔 → 免費

6. 唔 → 螞蟻

7. 唔 → 馬尾

8. 唔 → 美孚

9. 唔 → 美味

10. 唔 → 買餸

> **發共鳴聲時，要留意：**
>
> 1. 發聲是否輕鬆
> 2. 口腔及喉嚨是否放鬆
> 3. 感受嘴唇和門牙後方的振動
> 4. 字與字之間有否串聯起來
> 5. 聲線的清晰度

© Ma 2023. *Voice Therapy for Children: An Instructional Manual.*

筆記 11. 家居用聲練習：第 3 堂

完成每個練習項目後，於空格填上 "✓"，並給家長簽名。

家居練習	日期					
1. 每天喝六至八杯水 （約 1.5 至 2.0 公升）						
2. 注意聲線護理 （輕聲說話不大聲尖叫， 少吃刺激性食物等）						
3. 鬆弛運動和腹式呼吸 （每天練習兩遍）						
4. 共鳴聲練習 （每天練習兩遍，並把評分記錄 在筆記 12 和筆記 13 內）						
5. 為自己的聲線評分 （請把分數寫在空格內） 1 2 3 4 5 6 7 8 9 10						
家長簽名						

© Ma 2023. *Voice Therapy for Children: An Instructional Manual.*

筆記 12. 共鳴聲練習評分表（單字）

學生和家長輪流用共鳴聲讀出以下的單字，並互相為對方評分：

評分準則： 1. 輕鬆的發聲
2. 放鬆口腔及喉嚨
3. 感受嘴唇和門牙後方的振動
4. 哼聲與字有否串聯起來
5. 清晰的聲線

日期												
次數		1	2	1	2	1	2	1	2	1	2	1	2
唔 → 媽	學生												
	家長												
唔 → 咩	學生												
	家長												
唔 → 咪	學生												
	家長												
唔 → 麼	學生												
	家長												
唔 → 嗚	學生												
	家長												
唔 → 貓	學生												
	家長												
唔 → 芒	學生												
	家長												
唔 → 檬	學生												
	家長												
唔 → 麵	學生												
	家長												

© Ma 2023. *Voice Therapy for Children: An Instructional Manual.*

筆記 13. 共鳴聲練習評分表（詞語）

學生和家長輪流用共鳴聲讀出以下的詞語，並互相為對方評分：

評分準則：　1.　輕鬆的發聲
　　　　　　　2.　放鬆口腔及喉嚨
　　　　　　　3.　感受嘴唇和門牙後方的振動
　　　　　　　4.　字與字之間有否串聯起來
　　　　　　　5.　清晰的聲線

日期													
次數		1	2	1	2	1	2	1	2	1	2	1	2
唔 → 媽媽	學生												
	家長												
唔 → 芒果	學生												
	家長												
唔 → 貓咪	學生												
	家長												
唔 → 免費	學生												
	家長												
唔 → 螞蟻	學生												
	家長												
唔 → 馬尾	學生												
	家長												
唔 → 美孚	學生												
	家長												
唔 → 美味	學生												
	家長												
唔 → 買餸	學生												
	家長												

© Ma 2023. *Voice Therapy for Children: An Instructional Manual.*

筆記 14. 共鳴聲：句子

1. <u>媽媽</u>摸<u>貓</u>。

2. <u>媽媽</u>鍾意食<u>芒</u>果蛋糕。

3. <u>明明</u>住<u>美</u>孚。

4. 枱<u>面</u>有好多<u>螞</u>蟻。

5. <u>明明</u>鍾意表演<u>魔</u>術。

6. 今日科學館<u>免</u>費入場。

7. 動植<u>物</u>公園有<u>馬</u>騮睇。

8. 綁<u>馬</u>尾個<u>妹</u>妹跳<u>舞</u>好叻。

9. 我早餐食咗<u>饅</u>頭同炒<u>麵</u>。

10. <u>媽媽每晚</u>都睇電視。

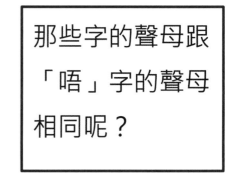

那些字的聲母跟「唔」字的聲母相同呢？

© Ma 2023. *Voice Therapy for Children: An Instructional Manual.*

筆記 15. 共鳴聲作句大挑戰

1. _____

2. _____

3. _____

4. _____

5. _____

6. _____

7. _____

8. _____

共鳴聲作句大挑戰——評分準則

1 至 2 句： ☺

3 至 4 句： ☺ ☺

5 句或以上： ☺ ☺ ☺

共鳴聲：

60–70% 時間放鬆： ☺

70–90% 時間放鬆： ☺ ☺

90–100% 時間放鬆： ☺ ☺ ☺

© Ma 2023. *Voice Therapy for Children: An Instructional Manual.*

筆記 16. 家居用聲練習：第 4 堂

完成每個練習項目後，於空格填上 "✓"，並給家長簽名。

家居練習	日期					
1.　每天喝六至八杯水 　　（約 1.5 至 2.0 公升）						
2.　注意聲線護理 　　（輕聲說話不大聲尖叫， 　　少吃刺激性食物等）						
3.　鬆弛運動和腹式呼吸 　　（每天練習兩遍）						
4.　共鳴聲練習 　　（每天練習兩遍，並把評分記錄 　　在筆記 17 內）						
5.　為自己的聲線評分 　　（請把分數寫在空格內） 　　1 2 3 4 5 6 7 8 9 10						
家長簽名						

© Ma 2023. *Voice Therapy for Children: An Instructional Manual.*

筆記 17. 共鳴聲練習評分表（句子）

用共鳴聲讀出以下的句子，並評分：

日期												
次數	1	2	1	2	1	2	1	2	1	2	1	2
1　唔→媽媽摸貓												
媽媽摸貓												
2　唔→媽媽鍾意食芒果蛋糕												
媽媽鍾意食芒果蛋糕												
3　唔→明明住美孚												
明明住美孚												
4　唔→枱面有好多螞蟻												
枱面有好多螞蟻												
5　唔→明明鍾意表演魔術												
明明鍾意表演魔術												
6　唔→今日科學館免費入場												
今日科學館免費入場												
7　唔→動植物公園有馬騮睇												
動植物公園有馬騮睇												
8　唔→綁馬尾個妹妹跳舞好叻												
綁馬尾個妹妹跳舞好叻												
9　唔→我早餐食咗饅頭同炒麵												
我早餐食咗饅頭同炒麵												
10　唔→媽媽每晚都睇電視												
媽媽每晚都睇電視												

© Ma 2023. *Voice Therapy for Children: An Instructional Manual.*

筆記18. 共鳴聲練習 + 聲線放送

比本領

月亮和太陽比本領，月亮說：「我在黑夜放光明，我的本領大。」

太陽說：「我在白天放光明，我的本領比你大。」

黑雲說：「我走出來，把你們都遮住了，還是我的本領大。」

比本領

（唔～）月亮和太陽比本領，

（唔～）月亮說：

（唔～）「我在黑夜放光明，

（唔～）我的本領大。」

（唔～）太陽說：

（唔～）「我在白天放光明，

（唔～）我的本領比你大。」

（唔～）黑雲說：

（唔～）「我走出來，

（唔～）把你們都遮住了，

（唔～）還是我的本領大。」

© Ma 2023. *Voice Therapy for Children: An Instructional Manual.*

筆記 19. 音量變化練習

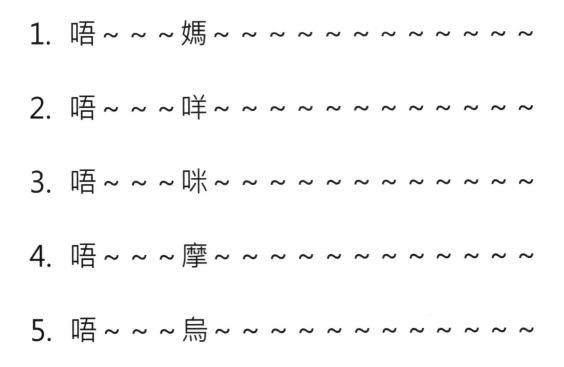

1. 唔～～～媽～～～～～～～～～～～～～

2. 唔～～～咩～～～～～～～～～～～～～

3. 唔～～～咪～～～～～～～～～～～～～

4. 唔～～～摩～～～～～～～～～～～～～

5. 唔～～～烏～～～～～～～～～～～～～

© Ma 2023. *Voice Therapy for Children: An Instructional Manual.*

筆記 20. 家居用聲練習：第 5 堂

完成每個練習項目後，於空格填上 "✓" ，並給家長簽名。

家居練習	日期					
1. 每天喝六至八杯水 （約 1.5 至 2.0 公升）						
2. 注意聲線護理 （輕聲說話不大聲尖叫，少吃刺激性食物等）						
3. 鬆弛運動和腹式呼吸 （每天練習兩遍）						
4. 每天用共鳴聲和家人聊天，討論當天發生的事，或感興趣的事物						
5. 與家人練習放鬆喉嚨用響亮的共鳴聲說話（例：把家中的電視稍為調大聲點然後和家人交談 / 與家人玩「老師話」/「狐狸先生幾多點」等遊戲）						
6. 為自己的聲線評分						
家長簽名						

© Ma 2023. *Voice Therapy for Children: An Instructional Manual.*

筆記 21. 家居用聲練習：第 6 堂

完成每個練習項目後，於空格填上 "✓" ，並給家長簽名。

家居練習	日期					
1. 每天喝六至八杯水（約 1.5 至 2.0 公升）						
2. 注意聲線護理（輕聲說話不大聲尖叫，少吃刺激性食物等）						
3. 鬆弛運動和腹式呼吸（每天練習兩遍）						
4. 每天用共鳴聲和家人聊天，討論當天發生的事，或感興趣的事物						
5. 與家人練習放鬆喉嚨用響亮的共鳴聲說話（例：把家中的電視稍為調大聲點然後和家人交談 / 與家人玩「老師話」/「狐狸先生幾多點」等遊戲）						
6. 為自己的聲線評分						
家長簽名						

© Ma 2023. *Voice Therapy for Children: An Instructional Manual.*

筆記 22. 我的聲線保護計劃

病了怎麼辦？

小朋友，如果你生病了，或遇到喉嚨痛、聲沙或失聲等問題，你會做甚麼去讓聲音早日復原呢？

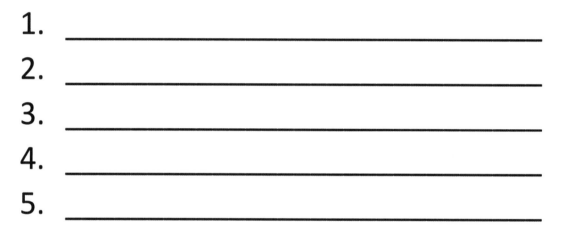

1. _____
2. _____
3. _____
4. _____
5. _____

© Ma 2023. *Voice Therapy for Children: An Instructional Manual.*

圖 1. 發聲原理

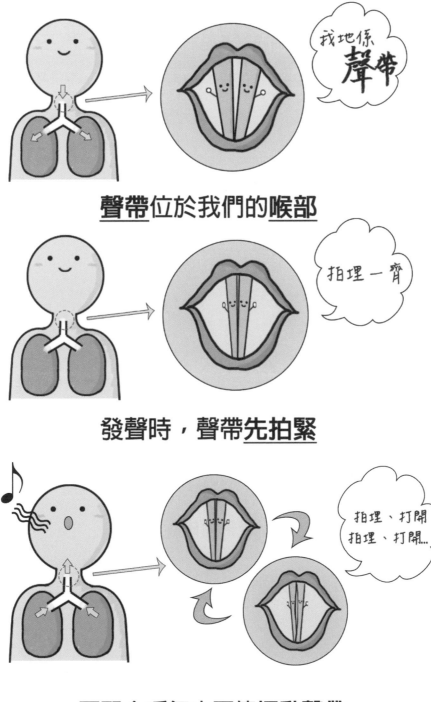

聲帶位於我們的喉部

發聲時，聲帶先拍緊

再配合呼氣去不停振動聲帶，
發出聲音

© Ma 2023. *Voice Therapy for Children: An Instructional Manual.*

圖 2. 聲帶生病了

長時間**不適當**地運用聲線，聲帶有機會**受損**，變得**紅腫**，這情況下，聲音會變得**沙啞**，說話時喉部或會感到**痛楚**。

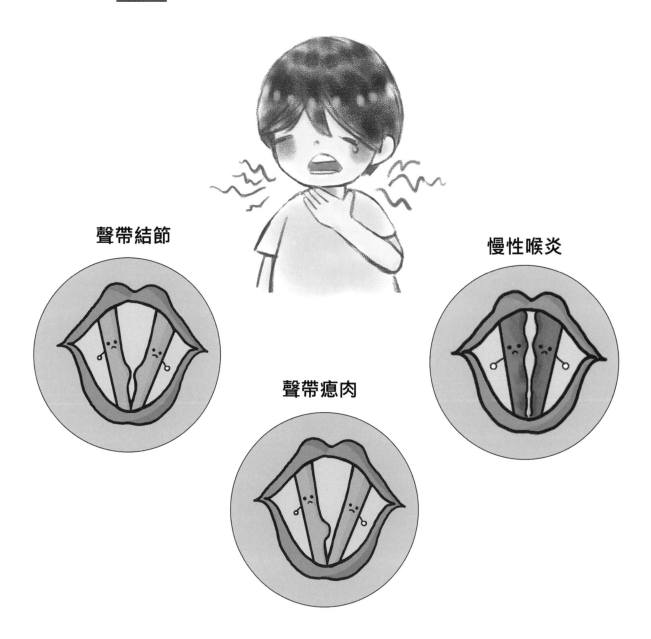

聲帶結節

聲帶瘜肉

慢性喉炎

© Ma 2023. *Voice Therapy for Children: An Instructional Manual.*

圖 3. 聲線評分表

© Ma 2023. *Voice Therapy for Children: An Instructional Manual.*

圖 4. 聲帶護理小百科

要多做

輕聲說話 ✕

多飲水

多放鬆自我

讓聲線得到充足休息

多休息

減少吃刺激性食物 ✕

放慢說話速度

並減少

長時間不停的用聲

經常大聲說話

在嘈吵環境大聲說話

說話急速

經常清喉嚨

吃大量辣、煎炸等刺激性食物

經常大力咳嗽

© Ma 2023. *Voice Therapy for Children: An Instructional Manual.*

圖 5. 鬆弛運動

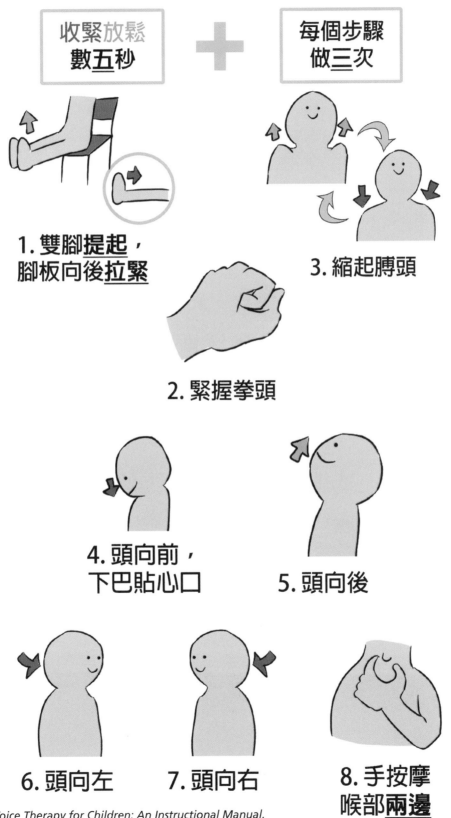

收緊放鬆
數五秒
┼
每個步驟
做三次

1. 雙腳提起，
腳板向後拉緊

2. 緊握拳頭

3. 縮起膊頭

4. 頭向前，
下巴貼心口

5. 頭向後

6. 頭向左

7. 頭向右

8. 手按摩
喉部兩邊

© Ma 2023. *Voice Therapy for Children: An Instructional Manual.*

圖 6. 腹式呼吸

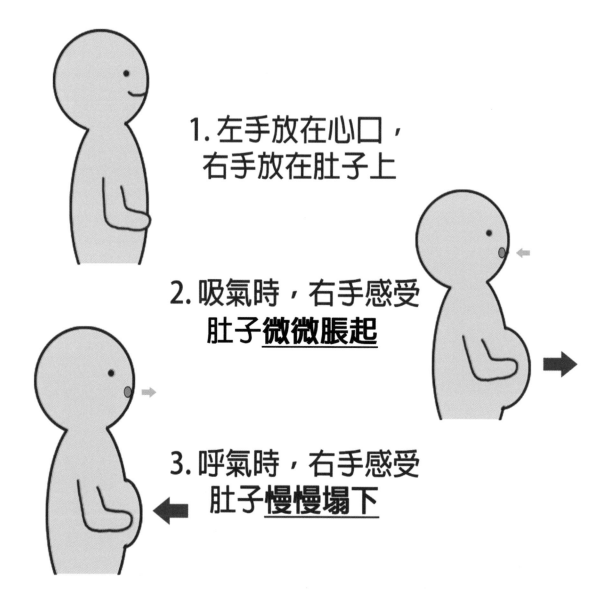

1. 左手放在心口，右手放在肚子上

2. 吸氣時，右手感受肚子**微微脹起**

3. 呼氣時，右手感受肚子**慢慢塌下**

© Ma 2023. *Voice Therapy for Children: An Instructional Manual.*

圖 7. 發聲位置圖

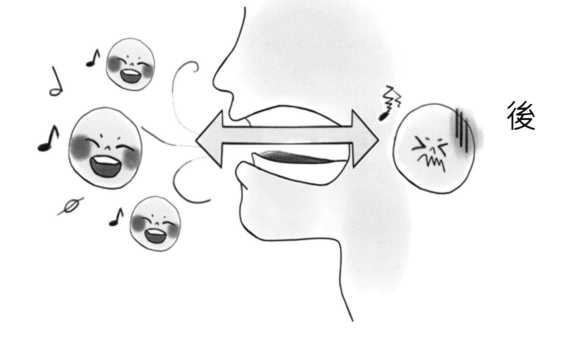

前

後

© Ma 2023. *Voice Therapy for Children: An Instructional Manual.*

圖 8. 詞語遊戲卡

毛巾	名字	麼-麼- 麼-麼-	咪-咪- 咩-咩-	媽-咩- 咪-麼-
抹枱	夢想	咪-咪- 咪-咪-	媽-媽- 麼-麼-	咩-咩- 咪-咪-
媽媽	鰻魚	咩-咩- 咩-咩-	媽-咪- 媽-咪-	moo-麼- moo-麼-
問題	饅頭	媽-媽- 媽-媽-	moo-moo- moo-moo-	咪-麼- 咪-麼-

螞蟻	買餸	魔術	舞蹈	蜜糖
馬騮	美味	買賣	玫瑰	蜜蜂
貓咪	美孚	碼頭	免費	網球
芒果	馬尾	滿足	麵包	味道

© Ma 2023. *Voice Therapy for Children: An Instructional Manual.*

Stimulus Cards

(Color version of the stimulus cards can be accessed by scanning the QR code below.)